CW01180343

Adventures in Numeracy

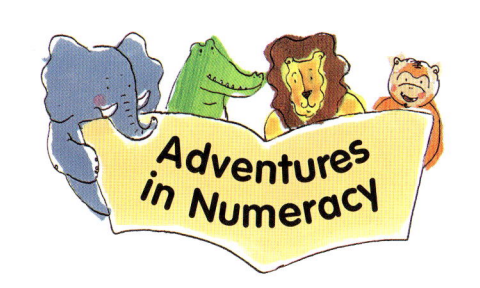

The Number Team have a Party

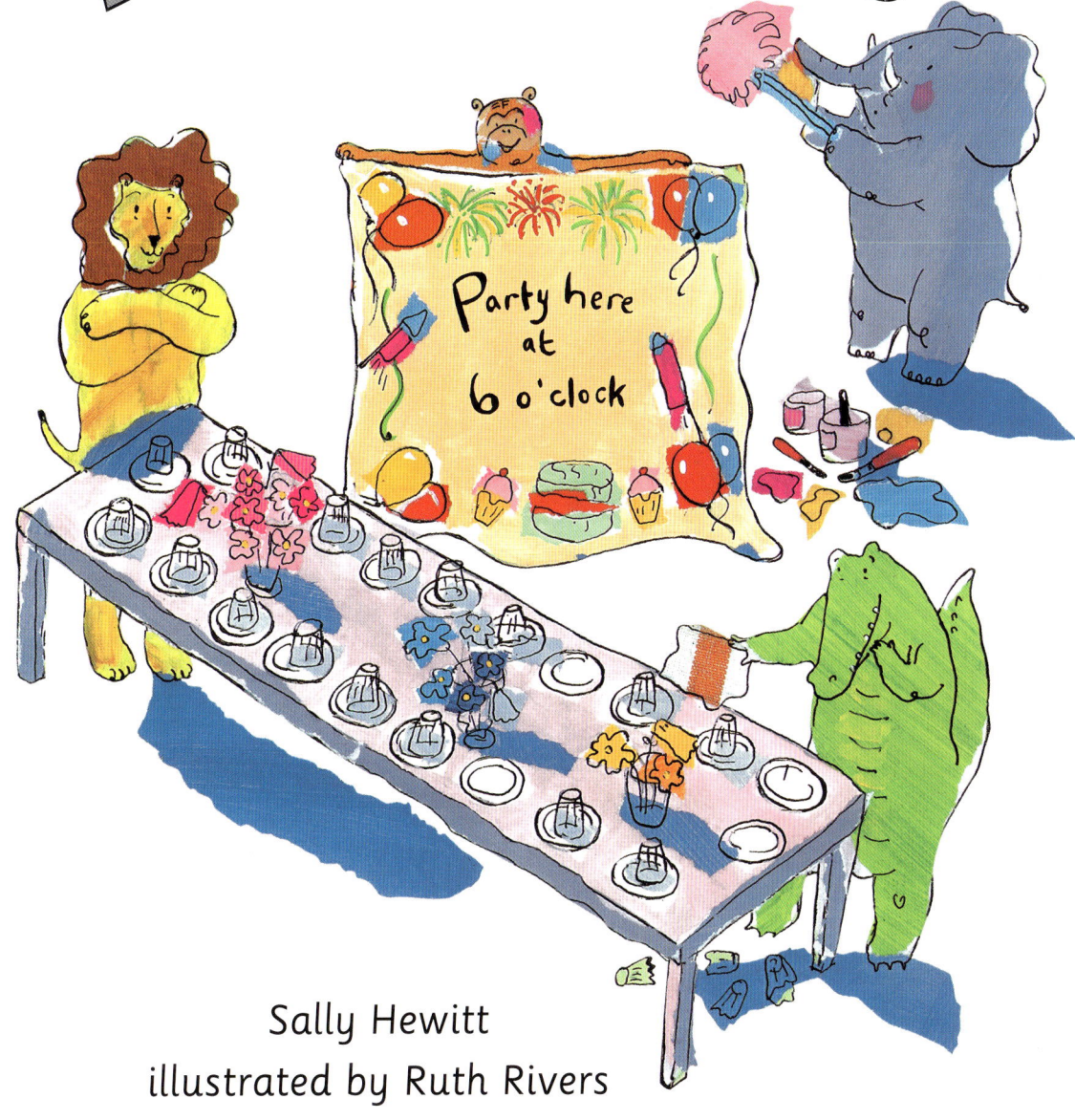

Party here at 6 o'clock

Sally Hewitt
illustrated by Ruth Rivers

Belitha Press

Notes for parents and teachers
How to use this book

Each double page has a numeracy theme, such as multiples, shapes or telling the time.

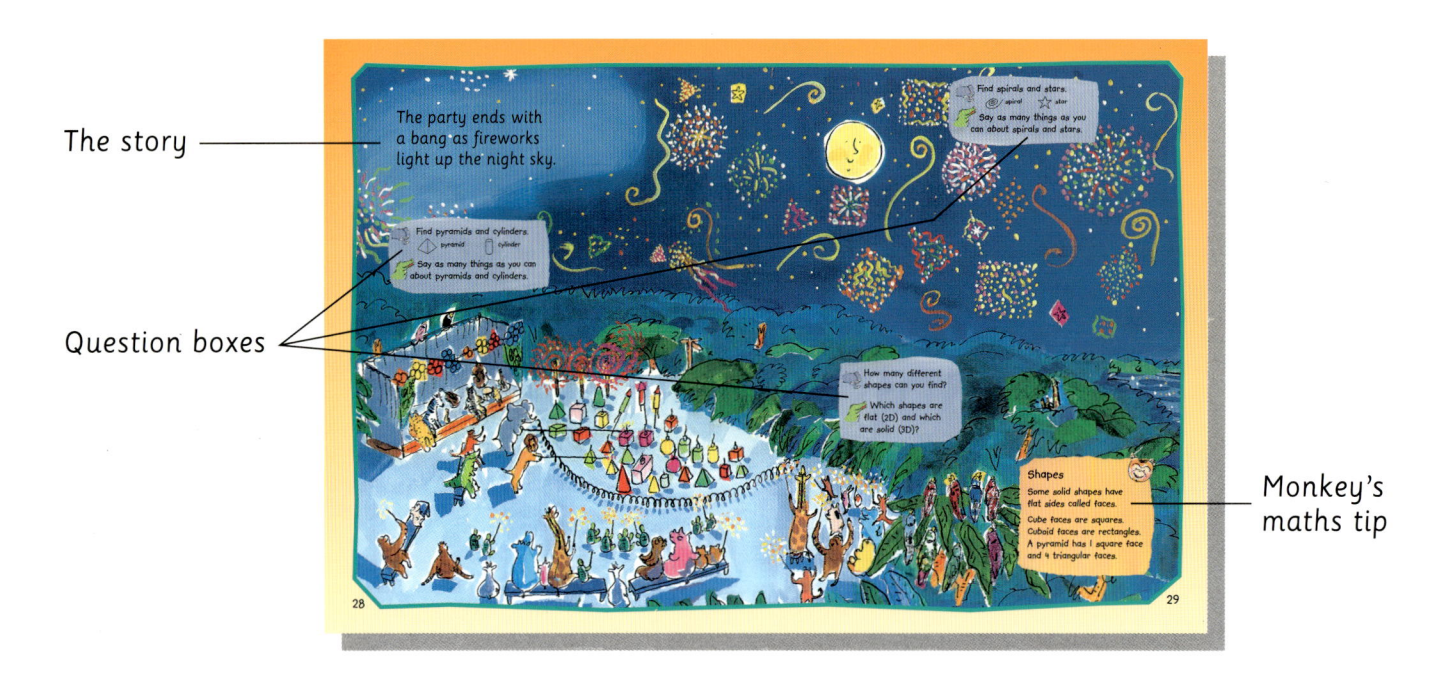

The story

Question boxes

Monkey's maths tip

Question boxes

Each box has two questions. Elephant's questions are easier than Crocodile's. Start with Elephant's questions, then move on to Crocodile's. Or you can choose to answer only Elephant's or only Crocodile's questions. The answers are on page 30.

Monkey's maths tip

Read Monkey's maths tip for help with the Number Team's questions, or extra information about the maths in the scene.

There are ideas for games and activities on page 31.

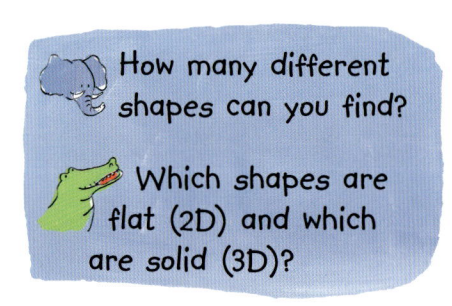

How many different shapes can you find?

Which shapes are flat (2D) and which are solid (3D)?

Shapes

Some solid shapes have flat sides called faces.

Cube faces are squares.
Cuboid faces are rectangles.
A pyramid has 1 square face and 4 triangular faces.

Meet the Number Team

Crocodile, Lion, Monkey and Elephant are throwing a party in the jungle – with a feast, dancing, games and fireworks. They need your help to make sure everything will be ready on time!

First the team deliver the party invitations. 'Don't get lost,' shouts Crocodile.

🐘 Follow the path to the banana trees.

🐊 Give Monkey directions to the banana trees.

Giving directions

When you give directions, it often helps to use a marker. For example:
- Turn right at the signpost.
- Cross the river at the stepping stones.
- Turn left at the tall tree.

First published in the UK in 2000 by

Belitha Press Limited, London House,
Great Eastern Wharf, Parkgate Road,
London SW11 4NQ

Copyright © Belitha Press Limited 2000
Text copyright © Sally Hewitt 2000
Illustrations by Ruth Rivers

Series editor: Mary-Jane Wilkins
Editor: Russell McLean
Designer: John Jamieson
Educational consultant: Norma Penny, Headteacher,
   Barnett Wood Infant School, Ashtead, Surrey

All rights reserved. No part of this book may
be reproduced or utilized in any form or by
any means, electronic or mechanical, including
photocopying, recording or by any information
storage and retrieval system, without permission
in writing from the publisher, except by a reviewer
who may quote brief passages in review.

ISBN 1 84138 235 3 (hardback)
ISBN 1 84138 239 6 (paperback)

Printed in China

British Library Cataloguing in Publication Data
for this book is available from the British Library.

10 9 8 7 6 5 4 3 2 1

Notes for parents and teachers
Games and activities

Use the Number Team's questions to help you find more maths in the pictures. Then try these games and activities.

4–5 Giving directions

Draw a map of your journey from home to school. Give a friend directions from one place on the map to another. Can they follow the route on the map?

8–9 Weighing and capacity

Make hot chocolate for one person. In a mug, add 200ml of hot (but not boiling) milk to 3 teaspoons of drinking chocolate, and stir until dissolved. How much milk and drinking chocolate are needed for 2, 3 or 4 people?

12–13 Sorting

Make some sandwiches for your friends. Find a way of recording information about what everyone wants, such as: brown or white bread; cheese or peanut butter filling. Make the sandwiches to order.

14–15 Telling the time

Make a set of 24 blank cards. Choose 6 different times. Draw each time on 4 cards: on 2 cards draw a clock with hands, on one card a digital clock, and on the 4th write the time in words. Use the cards to play snap and pairs.

18–19 Odd and even numbers

Fold a long strip of paper into a concertina. On the front fold draw a figure, with arms touching both edges. Cut it out to make a line of figures. Number them, using red for odd and blue for even numbers.

22–23 Guess and check

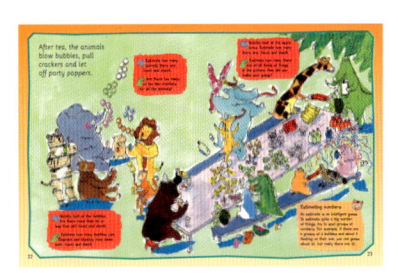

Put coloured beads in a see-through plastic pot, draw a starry sky, or build a castle with wooden bricks. Ask friends to guess the number of beads, stars and bricks. Who makes the most accurate guess?

26–27 Position

Hide treasure around a room. Write its position on cards – under a small table, behind the left curtain, and so on. Friends take a card, find the treasure, then collect another card. How much treasure did everyone find?

28–29 Shapes

Draw or paint a picture of a party, a firework display or a carnival. See how many different 2D and 3D shapes you can include in your picture.

Answers

Elephant and Crocodile ask both open and closed questions. Closed questions have just one correct answer. Open questions have a number of different correct answers. These will encourage your child to think of alternative answers and, in some cases, to count all the different possibilities.

4–5 Giving directions

- See answer to Crocodile's question below.
- One route: right at signpost, left at pig, right at zebra, cross bridge, right at tall tree, straight on at signpost, then cross bridge.

- See answer to Crocodile's question below.
- One route: straight on at signpost, right at pink flowers, left at puddle, left at butterflies, left at turtle, cross bridge, then left at giraffe.

- One route: straight on at signpost, right at pink flowers, left at puddle, straight on at butterflies, over stepping stones, straight on at tall tree, then left at signpost.
- One route back for Monkey: cross bridge, go past signpost, straight on at tall tree, cross stepping stones, past butterflies, past puddle, left at flowers, then straight past signpost.

6–7 Multiples

- 9 melons.
- 18, 15, 12, 9, 6, 3, 0.

- 12 coconuts.
- 20, 16, 12, 8, 4, 0.

- 70 potatoes.
- 100 potatoes.

8–9 Weighing and capacity

- Taking away – the scales tip to the right. Adding – the scales tip to the left.
- 10 tomatoes.

- 6 full bowls. 18 empty bowls.
- 3 tubs of ice cream.

- The bowl of dark pink icing holds the most. The bowl of yellow icing holds the least.
- Dark pink bowl + cake next to Crocodile. Light pink bowl + cake next to green bowl. Green bowl + cake next to yellow bowl. Yellow bowl + cake to the right of dark pink bowl.

10–11 Patterns

- Orange cube, red cube, pink sphere, yellow cylinder, blue cylinder, yellow cylinder.
- No – 1 red cube, 1 yellow cylinder are missing.

- 3 flowers in the next vase.
- 3, 9, 6 and 3 flowers – because Crocodile is making a pattern counting down in threes.

- 4 yellow balloons in the next bunch.
- 4, 6, 8, 2 and 4 balloons – the pattern is counting up in twos, up to 8.

12–13 Sorting

- 4 guitars, 1 drum, 5 trumpets, 3 saxophones, 1 piano and 2 double basses.
- You could write out a table (see Monkey's maths tip). Or you could draw each instrument and write the numbers on the pictures.

- There are more trumpets (5).
- Drum and piano (1 of each).

- Blow into 8 (trumpets, saxophones). Don't blow into 8 (guitars, drum, piano, double basses).
- By colour; whether they have strings; whether they are hit; whether they are carried.

14–15 Telling the time

- Elephant has the longest time (1 hour).
- Elephant: 1 hour. Crocodile: 45 minutes. Monkey: 30 minutes. Lion: 15 minutes.

- Lion (15 minutes).
- 30 minutes longer.

- Long hand points to 12, short hand to 6.
- 6:00.

16–17 Measuring

- 2 more chimps.
- 4 more turtles.

- Giraffe, Baby Giraffe and Hippo are taller. Turtle, Goat and Baby Hippo are shorter.
- Wildebeest (tall), Baby Giraffe (taller), Giraffe (tallest).

- Eagle's wingspan is widest.
- Small Vulture (wide), Big Vulture (wider), Eagle (widest).

18–19 Odd and even numbers

- 2, 4, 6, 8, 10, 12, 14, 16, 18, 20.
- Even (the numbers divide exactly by 2).

- 1, 3, 5, 7, 9, 11, 13, 15, 17, 19.
- Odd (the numbers do not divide exactly by 2 – there is always 1 left over).

- The same – 10 gold and 10 silver hats.
- The same – 10 red and 10 yellow crackers.

20–21 Double and half

- 20 cakes.
- 40 cakes.

- 8 gold, 5 green, 3 brown glasses.
- Cut one roll in half and take off 2½ rolls.

- 5 bananas, 8 apples, 12 oranges.
- 10 bananas, 16 apples, 24 oranges.

22–23 Estimate and check

- 20 animals.
- There are too few crackers (12).

- There are more than 20 bubbles (27 in all).
- Elephant 16, Lion 9, Monkey 2.

- 12 apple cores.
- 10 banana skins, 14 blowers, 17 party poppers, 8 bowls. Look out for groups to help you guess.

24–25 Number stories

- Nine coconuts are on their stands, six have been knocked off. That makes fifteen in all.
- $15 - 6 = 9$.

- Crocodile is balancing five melons. Add four melons that he dropped, that makes nine.
- $5 + 4 = 9$.

- Lion is juggling six oranges and three bananas. That makes nine pieces of fruit in all.
- One number story is: four animals are racing on balloons. Take away one balloon which has burst, to leave three balloons ($4 - 1 = 3$).

26–27 Position and direction

- The circle to the left of Crocodile.
- The circle in front of the stage.

- The line led by a turtle.
- The line with Elephant, a chimp and a turtle.

- Tiger.
- One example: Lion is to the left of Wildebeest.

28–29 Shapes

- Some of the fireworks on the ground are pyramids and cylinders.
- Pyramid: solid (3D); the base is a square; the other faces are triangles. Cylinder: solid (3D); 3 faces; 2 of the faces are circles of equal size.

- There are spirals and stars in the sky.
- Spiral: a flat (2D) curve that winds round and round. Star: flat (2D) shape; straight edges; a star can have any number of points.

- Pyramids, cubes, cuboids, cylinders, spheres, cones (all on the ground). Spirals, stars, circles, triangles, squares, diamonds (all in the sky).
- 2D: spiral, star, circle, square, triangle, diamond. 3D: pyramid, cube, cuboid, cylinder, sphere, cone.

Find spirals and stars.

🌀 spiral   ☆ star

Say as many things as you can about spirals and stars.

How many different shapes can you find?

Which shapes are flat (2D) and which are solid (3D)?

Shapes

Some solid shapes have flat sides called faces.

Cube faces are squares.
Cuboid faces are rectangles.
A pyramid has 1 square face and 4 triangular faces.

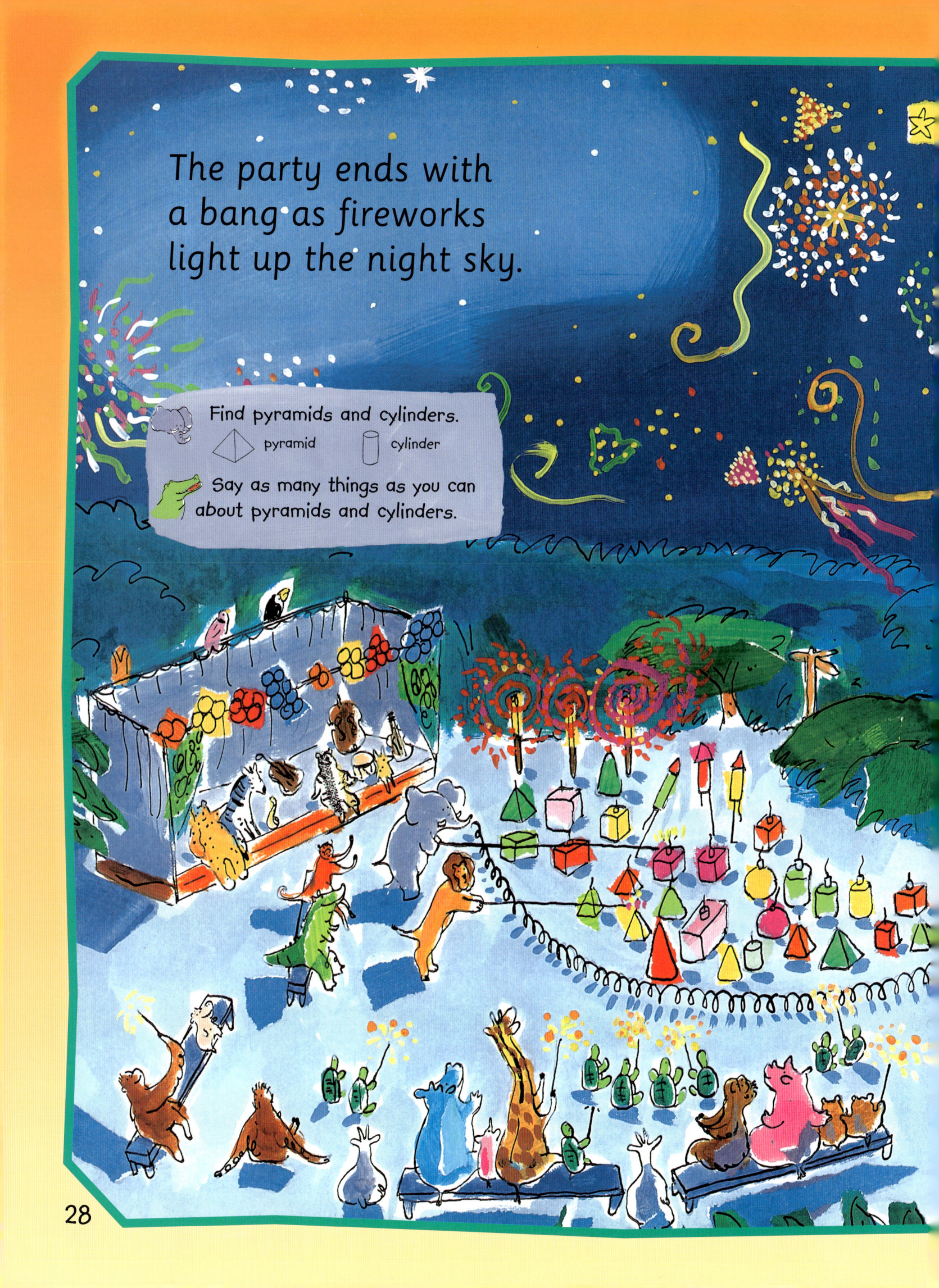

The party ends with a bang as fireworks light up the night sky.

Find pyramids and cylinders.
△ pyramid   ▯ cylinder

Say as many things as you can about pyramids and cylinders.

🐘 Find a line of animals moving forwards.

🐊 Find a line of animals moving backwards.

🐘 Find the animal who is between Monkey and Hippo.

🐊 Describe the position of an animal and ask a friend to guess which one it is.

Clockwise and anticlockwise

If you are going around the same way as the hands on a clock, you are going clockwise. If you are going the opposite way, you are going anticlockwise.

27

After the games the animals dance to the band. 'Watch out!' cries Elephant.

> Which circle of dancers is going round the same way as the hands on a clock?
>
> Which circle of dancers is going round the opposite way to the hands on a clock?

26

Make up a number story about the bananas and oranges that Lion is juggling.

Make up number stories from all sorts of things in the picture.

Number stories

A mathematical story uses numbers and symbols. A number story can be told in words. For example, six turtles have jumped on Elephant. Add the two who are waiting to make eight.

The calculation for this is 6 + 2 = 8.

Lion juggles fruit while Monkey tries his luck at the coconut shy.

Can you see how the calculation 9 + 6 = 15 is a number story about the coconut shy?

Make up a number story about the coconuts without using the + sign.

Tell a number story in words about Crocodile's melons.

The calculation 9 − 4 = 5 tells the story of Crocodile's melons. Find a different calculation to tell the story.

🐘 Quickly look at the apple cores. Estimate how many there are. Count and check.

🐊 Estimate how many there are of all kinds of things in the picture. How did you make your guess?

Estimating numbers

An estimate is an intelligent guess. To estimate quite a big number of things, try to spot groups of numbers. For example, if there are 4 groups of 5 bubbles and about 3 floating on their own, you can guess about 20, but really there are 23.

23

After tea, the animals blow bubbles, pull crackers and let off party poppers.

Estimate how many animals there are. Count and check.

Are there too many or too few crackers for all the animals?

Quickly look at the bubbles. Are there more than 20 or less than 20? Count and check.

Estimate how many *bubbles* Lion, Elephant and Monkey have blown each. Count and check.

Halve the number of glasses on each of Elephant's trays.

What will Crocodile have to do to halve the number of rolls on his plate?

How many apples, oranges and bananas is Monkey carrying?

Can you double the number of Monkey's apples, oranges and bananas?

21

Some of the guests can't wait for the food to be served. What a feast!

How many cakes will Lion have on his plate if he doubles the number?

Can you double the number of all the small pink cakes?

Double and half

To halve a number, divide it exactly into 2. If it is an odd number, cut the 1 left over in half! So half of 7 is $3\frac{1}{2}$.

To double a number, add exactly the same number to it. So 4 + 4 = 8.

Odd and even numbers

An even number divides exactly by 2. When an odd number is divided by 2, there is always just 1 left over.

So 6 is an even number because it divides exactly by 2, into 3 and 3.

7 is an odd number because it does not divide exactly by 2 – there is 1 left over.

Estimate whether the number of gold hats is the same as the number of silver hats.

Estimate whether the number of red crackers is the same as the number of yellow crackers. Count them to check if you were right.

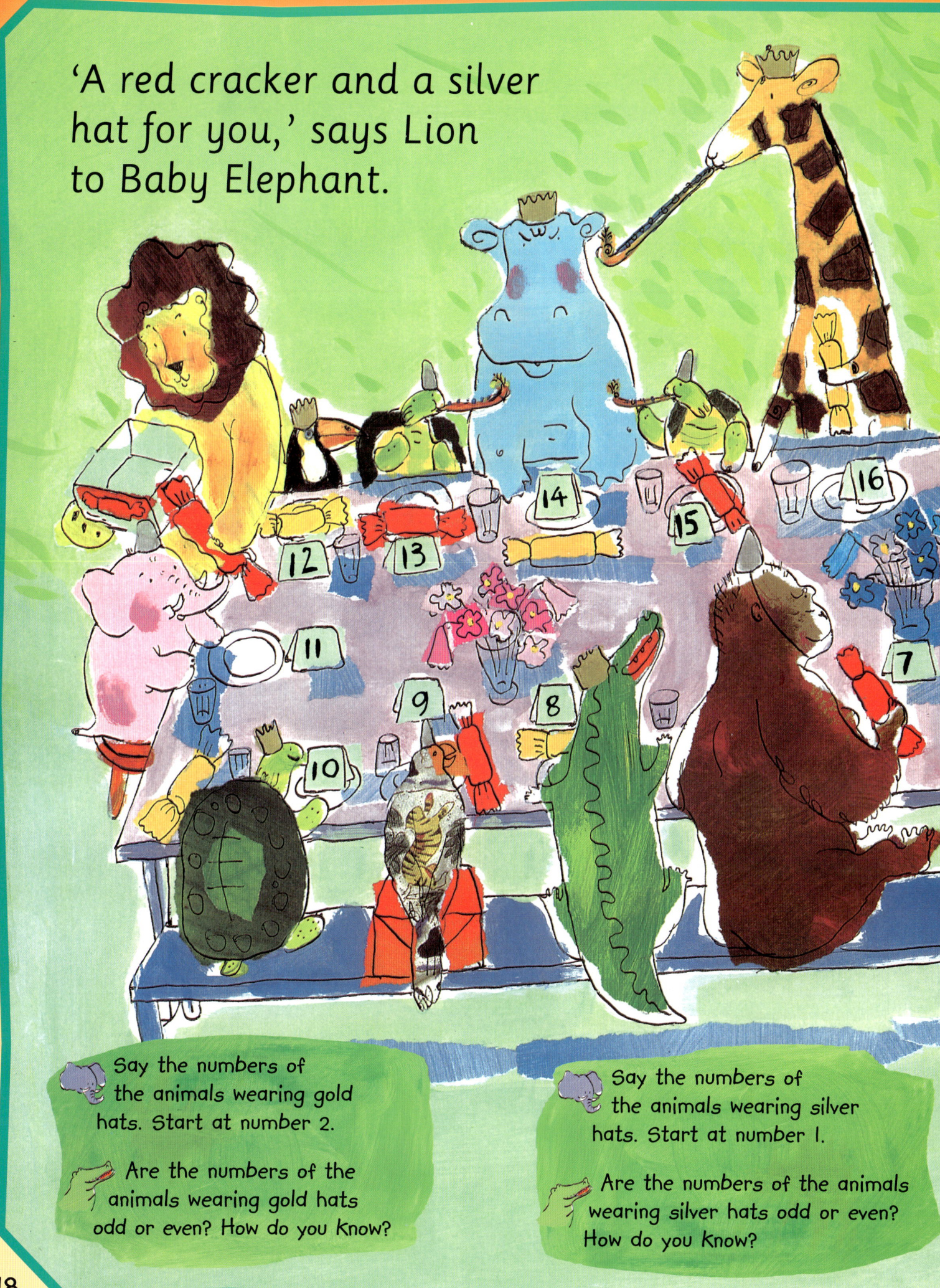

'A red cracker and a silver hat for you,' says Lion to Baby Elephant.

- Say the numbers of the animals wearing gold hats. Start at number 2.
- Are the numbers of the animals wearing gold hats odd or even? How do you know?

- Say the numbers of the animals wearing silver hats. Start at number 1.
- Are the numbers of the animals wearing silver hats odd or even? How do you know?

Measuring

When you measure how long, how wide or how high something is, you need to use a ruler or a tape measure to be accurate. Usually when you use a ruler, you measure in centimetres.

high
wide
long

Which bird's wingspan is the widest?

Find 3 birds whose wingspans are wide, wider and widest.

Party here at 6 o'clock

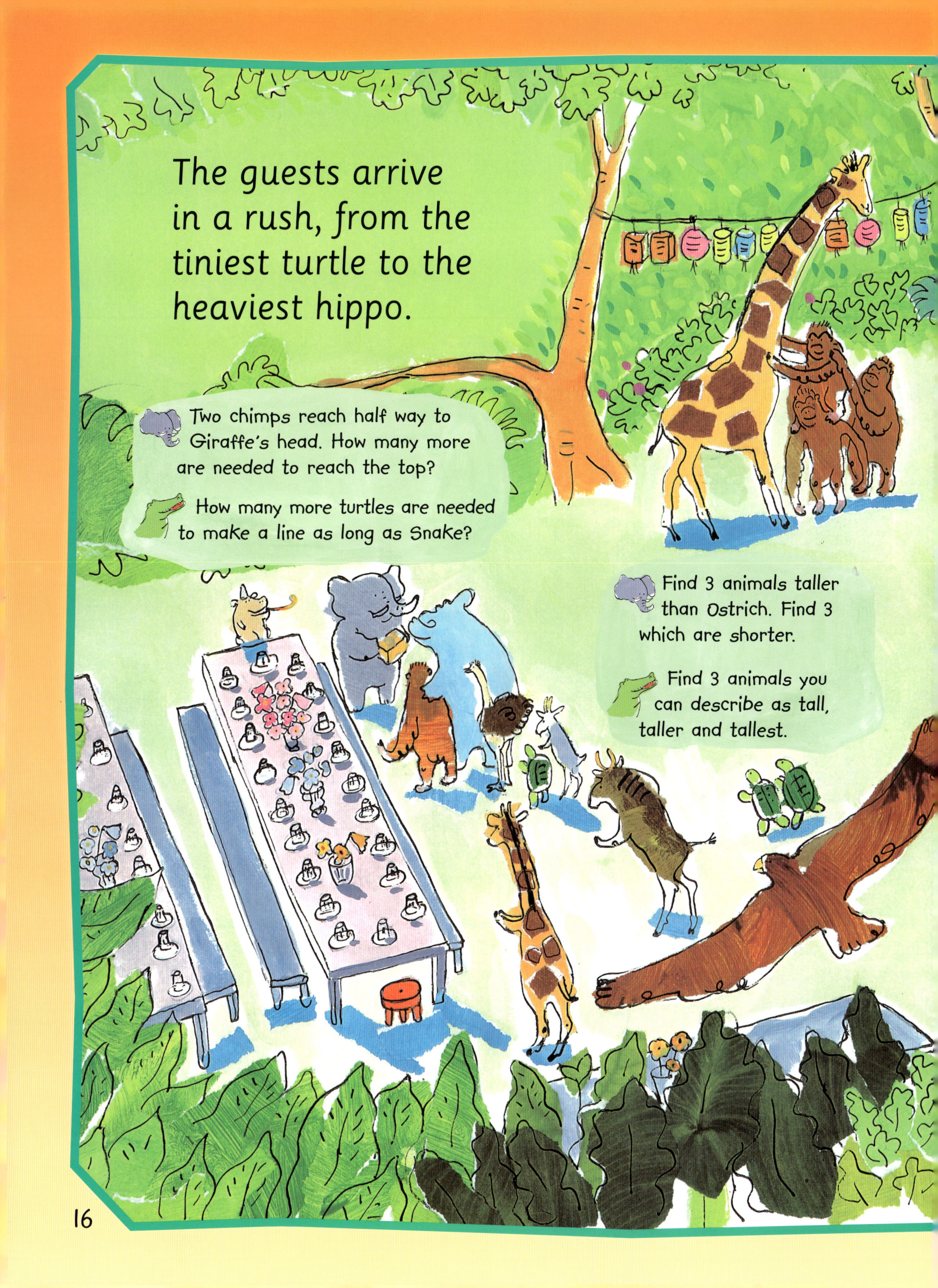

The guests arrive in a rush, from the tiniest turtle to the heaviest hippo.

Two chimps reach half way to Giraffe's head. How many more are needed to reach the top?

How many more turtles are needed to make a line as long as Snake?

Find 3 animals taller than Ostrich. Find 3 which are shorter.

Find 3 animals you can describe as tall, taller and tallest.

Party here at 6 o'clock

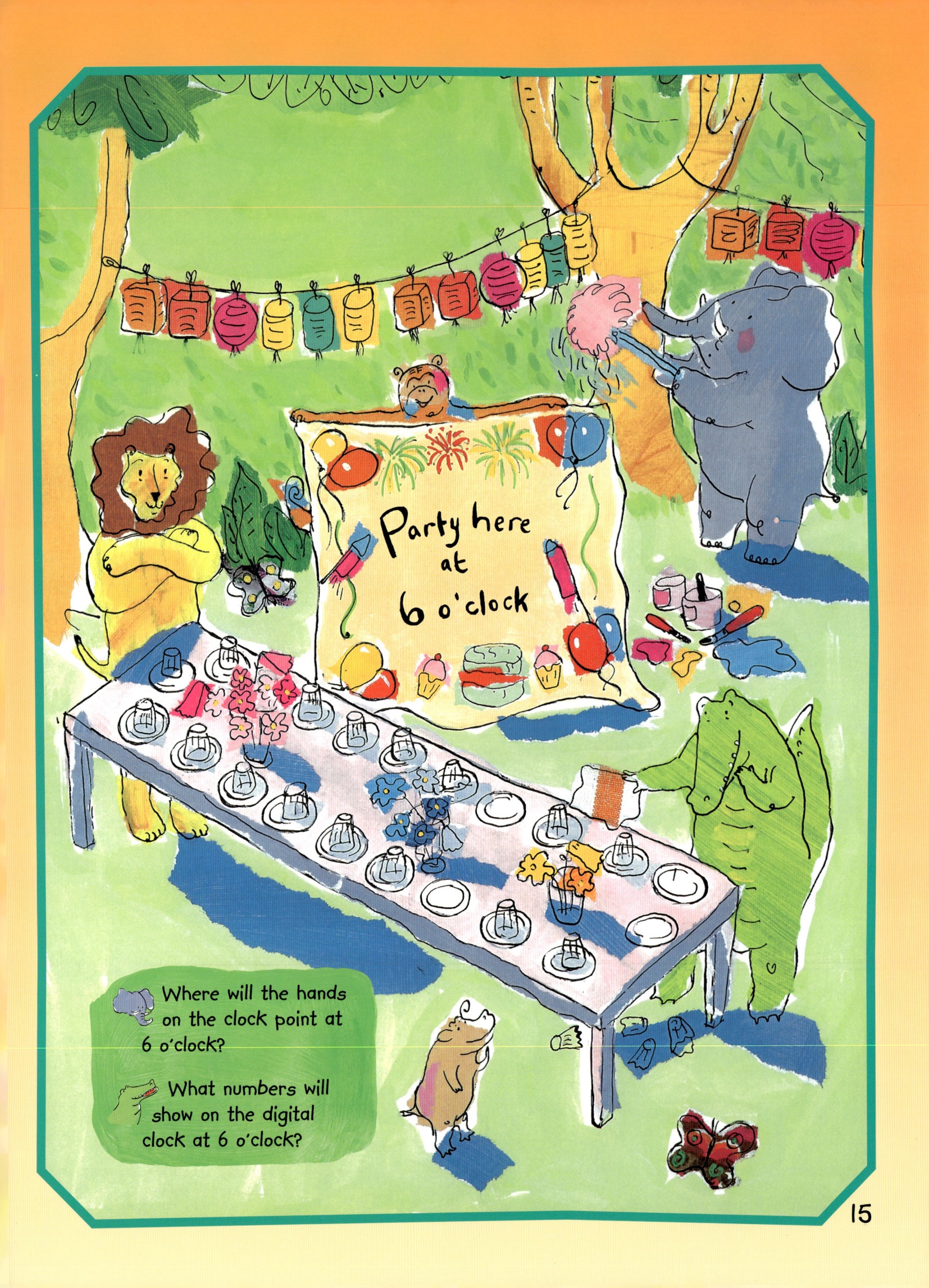

- Where will the hands on the clock point at 6 o'clock?
- What numbers will show on the digital clock at 6 o'clock?

'Hurry up, the party starts at six o'clock,' shouts Crocodile.

Telling the time

Counting in fifteens helps you to tell the time.

There are 60 minutes in an hour.

15 minutes is a quarter of an hour.

30 minutes is half an hour.

45 minutes is three-quarters of an hour.

5:00

5:15

The animals start their jobs at different times. Who has the longest time to finish?

How long does everyone have to finish their jobs before the party starts?

5:30

Who has the shortest time to finish their job before the party starts?

How much more time has Crocodile to finish his job than Lion?

5:45

Count the instruments you blow into to play and those you don't blow into to play.

Think of as many ways as you can to sort the instruments.

There are more of one instrument than any other. Which one?

There are the same number of 2 instruments. Which are they?

13

The band arrives as Crocodile checks his list. 'Are all the musicians here?' he asks.

How many of each instrument are there in the band?

Think of 2 ways to record how many there are of each instrument.

Make a table

A table like this is a quick way of writing down information.

Balloons	Total
Orange	6
Yellow	8
Red	12
Blue	16

How many balloons should Monkey put in the next bunch?

How many balloons should there be in the next 5 bunches? How do you know?

Patterns

You can use a number square to make interesting number patterns.

On a hundred square, count on in twos. Colour the numbers you land on. Do the same with fives and tens.

Then try counting on in other numbers.

Lion and Monkey decorate the stage while Elephant hangs up lanterns.

Which 6 lanterns should Elephant hang up next?

Are there enough lanterns to make 2 more of the same pattern?

How many flowers should Crocodile put in the next empty vase?

How many flowers should there be in each of the 4 empty vases? How do you know?

Which bowl holds the most icing? Which bowl holds the least icing?

Match each cake to a bowl that holds the right amount of icing to cover it.

Measuring

Water and other liquids which you can pour are measured in litres. There are 1000 millilitres in 1 litre.

Solid things such as potatoes, sugar or flour are measured in kilograms. There are 1000 grams in 1 kilogram.

'Did we buy enough ice cream to fill all these bowls?' wonders Elephant.

What will happen to the scales if Monkey takes one tomato off? What will happen if she adds an extra tomato?

How many tomatoes balance with 2 potatoes?

How many full bowls of ice cream are there? How many empty bowls?

One tub of ice cream fills 6 bowls. How many tubs are needed to fill the empty bowls?

Count in fours to find how many coconuts Monkey has bought.

There were 20 coconuts on the stall to start with. Start at 20 and count backwards in fours until you reach zero. What numbers do you say?

There are 10 potatoes in each bag. Count in tens to find how many potatoes Crocodile has bought.

Work out how many potatoes there were on the stall to start with if there are 10 potatoes in each bag.

Multiples

A multiple of 10 is a number that has been multiplied by 10. So 20, 30, 40 and 50 are all multiples of 10. All multiples of 10 end in 0.

Multiples of 5 end in 0 or 5.

Multiples of 2 end in 0, 2, 4, 6 or 8.

Next the team buy food for the feast. 'These potatoes are heavy,' puffs Crocodile.

Count in threes to find how many melons Lion has bought.

There were 18 melons on the stall. Start at 18 and count backwards in threes to zero. What numbers do you say?

- Follow the path to the lake.
- Give Elephant directions to the lake.

- Give Lion directions to the rocky hills.
- Give directions to Monkey, Elephant and Lion so that they can get back to Crocodile.